HIP-HOP

Alicia Keys	Lil Wayne
Ashanti	LL Cool J
Beyoncé	Lloyd Banks
Black Eyed Peas	Ludacris
Busta Rhymes	Mariah Carey
Chris Brown	Mary J. Blige
Christina Aguilera	Missy Elliot
Ciara	Nas
Cypress Hill	Nelly
Daddy Yankee	Notorious B.I.G.
DMX	OutKast
Don Omar	Pharrell Williams
Dr. Dre	Pitbull
Eminem	Queen Latifah
Fat Joe	Reverend Run (of Run DMC)
50 Cent	Sean "Diddy" Combs
The Game	Snoop Dogg
Hip-Hop: A Short History	T.I.
Hip-Hop Around the World	Tupac
Ice Cube	Usher
Ivy Queen	Will Smith
Jay-Z	Wu-Tang Clan
Jennifer Lopez	Xzibit
Juelz Santana	Young Jeezy
Kanye West	Yung Joc

Daddy Yankee has helped bring reggaeton to the world's attention.

Daddy Yankee

Nat Cotts

Mason Crest Publishers

Daddy Yankee

Copyright © 2008 by Mason Crest Publishers. All rights reserved. No part of this publication may be reproduced or transmitted in any form or by any means, electronic or mechanical, including photocopying, recording, taping, or any information storage and retrieval system, without permission from the publisher.

Produced by Harding House Publishing Service, Inc.
201 Harding Avenue, Vestal, NY 13850.

MASON CREST PUBLISHERS INC.
370 Reed Road
Broomall, Pennsylvania 19008
(866)MCP-BOOK (toll free)
www.masoncrest.com

Printed in the United States of America

First Printing

9 8 7 6 5 4 3 2 1

Library of Congress Cataloging-in-Publication Data

Cotts, Nat.
  Daddy Yankee / Nat Cotts.
     p. cm. — (Hip-hop)
  Includes bibliographical references and index.
  ISBN 978-1-4222-0288-3
  ISBN: 978-1-4222-0077-3 (series)
  1. Daddy Yankee—Juvenile literature. 2. Rap musicians—Puerto Rico—Biography—Juvenile literature. I. Title.
  ML3930.D25C68 2008
  782.421649092—dc22
  [B]
                                    2007028142

Publisher's notes:
• All quotations in this book come from original sources and contain the spelling and grammatical inconsistencies of the original text.

• The Web sites mentioned in this book were active at the time of publication. The publisher is not responsible for Web sites that have changed their addresses or discontinued operation since the date of publication. The publisher will review and update the Web site addresses each time the book is reprinted.

DISCLAIMER: The following story has been thoroughly researched, and to the best of our knowledge, represents a true story. While every possible effort has been made to ensure accuracy, the publisher will not assume liability for damages caused by inaccuracies in the data, and makes no warranty on the accuracy of the information contained herein. This story has not been authorized nor endorsed by Daddy Yankee.

Contents

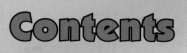

Hip-Hop Time Line

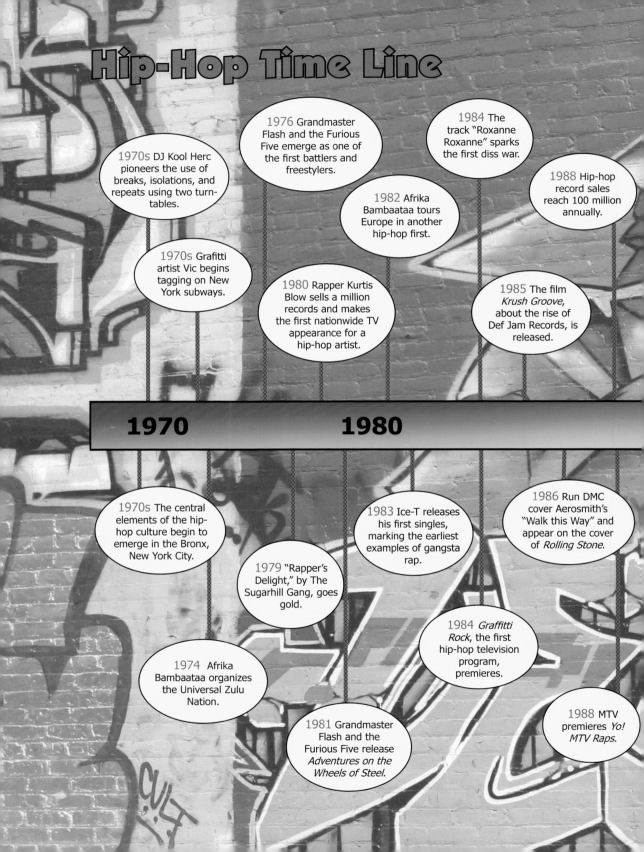

1976 Grandmaster Flash and the Furious Five emerge as one of the first battlers and freestylers.

1984 The track "Roxanne Roxanne" sparks the first diss war.

1970s DJ Kool Herc pioneers the use of breaks, isolations, and repeats using two turn-tables.

1988 Hip-hop record sales reach 100 million annually.

1982 Afrika Bambaataa tours Europe in another hip-hop first.

1970s Grafitti artist Vic begins tagging on New York subways.

1980 Rapper Kurtis Blow sells a million records and makes the first nationwide TV appearance for a hip-hop artist.

1985 The film *Krush Groove*, about the rise of Def Jam Records, is released.

1970   1980

1970s The central elements of the hip-hop culture begin to emerge in the Bronx, New York City.

1983 Ice-T releases his first singles, marking the earliest examples of gangsta rap.

1986 Run DMC cover Aerosmith's "Walk this Way" and appear on the cover of *Rolling Stone*.

1979 "Rapper's Delight," by The Sugarhill Gang, goes gold.

1984 *Graffitti Rock*, the first hip-hop television program, premieres.

1974 Afrika Bambaataa organizes the Universal Zulu Nation.

1988 MTV premieres *Yo! MTV Raps*.

1981 Grandmaster Flash and the Furious Five release *Adventures on the Wheels of Steel*.

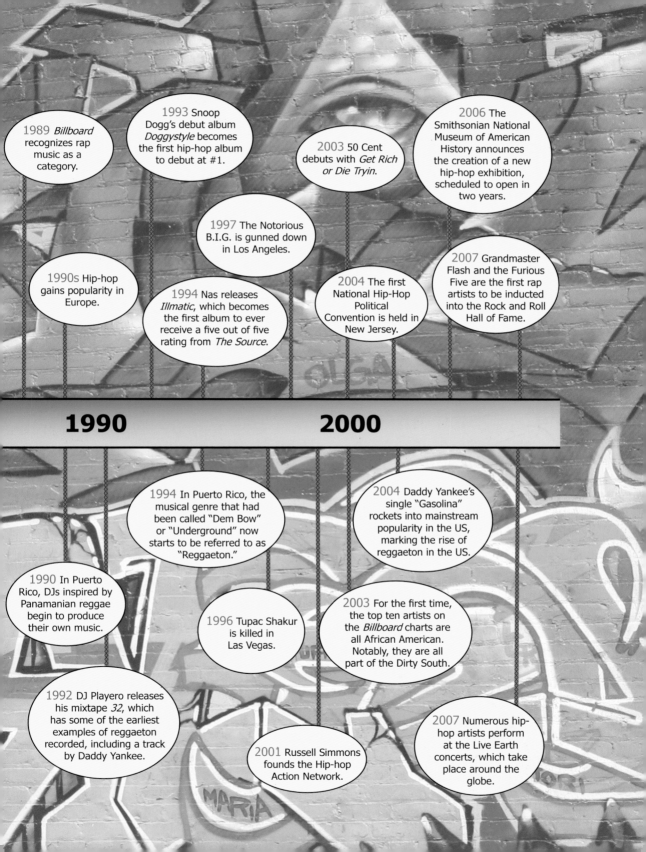

1989 *Billboard* recognizes rap music as a category.

1993 Snoop Dogg's debut album *Doggystyle* becomes the first hip-hop album to debut at #1.

2003 50 Cent debuts with *Get Rich or Die Tryin*.

2006 The Smithsonian National Museum of American History announces the creation of a new hip-hop exhibition, scheduled to open in two years.

1997 The Notorious B.I.G. is gunned down in Los Angeles.

1990s Hip-hop gains popularity in Europe.

1994 Nas releases *Illmatic*, which becomes the first album to ever receive a five out of five rating from *The Source*.

2004 The first National Hip-Hop Political Convention is held in New Jersey.

2007 Grandmaster Flash and the Furious Five are the first rap artists to be inducted into the Rock and Roll Hall of Fame.

1990

2000

1994 In Puerto Rico, the musical genre that had been called "Dem Bow" or "Underground" now starts to be referred to as "Reggaeton."

2004 Daddy Yankee's single "Gasolina" rockets into mainstream popularity in the US, marking the rise of reggaeton in the US.

1990 In Puerto Rico, DJs inspired by Panamanian reggae begin to produce their own music.

1996 Tupac Shakur is killed in Las Vegas.

2003 For the first time, the top ten artists on the *Billboard* charts are all African American. Notably, they are all part of the Dirty South.

1992 DJ Playero releases his mixtape *32*, which has some of the earliest examples of reggaeton recorded, including a track by Daddy Yankee.

2001 Russell Simmons founds the Hip-hop Action Network.

2007 Numerous hip-hop artists perform at the Live Earth concerts, which take place around the globe.

Daddy Yankee is not just a music megastar; he is the "poster boy" for an entire genre—reggaeton.

1

The Night

The Billboard Awards had never seen a performer like Daddy Yankee. In its thirty-eight-year history, the awards ceremony had seen many different acts and artists come and go—but at the 2005 ceremony, Daddy Yankee was something entirely new. He looked a little like a *gangsta rapper*, wearing a suit, sunglasses, and plenty of *bling*. But he wasn't . . . not quite, at least.

The Difference

Daddy Yankee did have plenty of things in common with gangsta rappers like Dr. Dre, the Wu-Tang Clan, or The Game. He too had grown up poor, surrounded by crime and drugs, and that experience shaped his music, giving him both the fire he needed to succeed and the subjects that inspired his songs. His album *Barrio Fino* had everything from party *anthems* to emotional calls for peace on the streets.

The album, in fact, was the reason he was at the Billboard Awards in the first place. Released only in July of the year before, the album had been nominated for multiple awards, including the important Best Latin Music Album of the Year. That one word—"Latin"—explains what separates Daddy Yankee from most of the other hip-hop artists who made it big before him: Daddy Yankee was not from Compton, California, or New York City's South Bronx; he wasn't even from the United States. Instead, when he came to the podium to give his acceptance speech as the winner, he spoke with an accent. His childhood in San Juan, Puerto Rico, flavored every word.

A New Kind of Music

On that night in 2005, as he stood on the podium holding the silver Billboard trophy, Daddy Yankee was the sign of things to come. His accent, his heritage, and his kind of music—reggaeton—were all signs of a new trend in music, one that spoke Spanish as its first language and danced to the beat of Jamaican dance halls mixed with Panamanian *salsa*. Reggaeton was a new kind of music, one that sounded a lot like hip-hop or rap. For Latinos both in and out of the United States, reggaeton was an important means of expression and identity, just as rap was for African Americans. And reggaeton was growing in popularity.

By the time Daddy Yankee stood on the podium, reggaeton had spread itself around the world. Clubs and stereos from Argentina to Germany and everywhere in between rocked to the rollicking beat of the new *genre*. Daddy Yankee had played a big part in spreading reggaeton all over the world. Despite the fact that he only rapped in the sharp, fast Spanish of Puerto Rico, the music he had crafted appealed to whoever heard it. The award that Daddy Yankee took home that night was for "Latin" music—but thanks to his craftsmanship, reggaeton had exploded beyond that label. It was now an international craze. And Daddy Yankee's music was just the beginning.

Leading the Way

Other reggaeton artists from Puerto Rico, the Dominican Republic, Mexico, and many other countries would soon follow with releases of their own albums in the United States and Europe. They would all be following in Daddy Yankee's

Influenced by hip-hop, reggae, and other forms of music, reggaeton won over its own group of fans with its high-energy beat. It's impossible not to move when reggaeton plays.

Daddy Yankee was born and raised in Puerto Rico, and he still lives there today. He is a symbol of some of the best the island nation has to offer.

footsteps, like explorers on a trail hacked through a South American jungle. As he stood on the podium that night, Daddy Yankee was not only an individual recording artist; he was also the machete that had cut a trail through the music world for an entire people, letting them claim a space that was entirely theirs.

In a way, as he stood on the podium that night, Daddy Yankee represented reggaeton itself: what it had become and what it could be. His story is really the story of the movement, of reggaeton's rise from its roots in American hip-hop and Caribbean dance to the awards podium that night and beyond. You might say Daddy Yankee is the soul of the genre. His childhood is what reggaeton artists sing about, and his career is the force behind the movement's explosion into the mainstream.

Reggaeton's Soul

There is no better artist for the role of reggaeton's soul than Daddy Yankee. He followed his 2005 Billboard Music Award with another the following year. He has also won Latin Grammy awards, including one for *Barrio Fino* in the Best Urban Music Album category. Meanwhile, his star status has reaped benefits beyond the world of music. Daddy Yankee is now the primary spokesman for Pepsi in all of Latin America, thanks to a lucrative promotion deal, and Reebok has recently launched a Daddy Yankee clothing line named DY. DY's first product is, of course, a shoe named for the reggaeton star, something that puts Daddy Yankee on the same level as Michael Jordan and Carmelo Anthony.

Yet, despite this success and the wealth and fame it has brought him, Daddy Yankee still is careful to stay true to himself and to his roots. It is this more than anything that keeps him connected to reggaeton's soul.

San Juan, the capital of Puerto Rico, is a beautiful, sprawling city. Ramón Ayala—Daddy Yankee—was born and raised in one of its less attractive, poverty-stricken barrios.

2

The Neighborhood

Daddy Yankee never gives the year of his birth. He was born on February 3, sometime in the late 1970s. He is, depending on whom you ask, twenty-eight, twenty-nine, or thirty. When he was born in the *barrio* of Las Lomas in Rio Piedras, Puerto Rico, part of the sprawling capital city of San Juan, his parents named him Ramón Ayala.

Life on the Streets

Daddy Yankee often talks about growing up as a child of the streets. Rio Piedras is the South Bronx of San Juan, with all the poverty, drugs, and crime of an urban ghetto under a baking Caribbean sun. Ramón grew up with his three siblings in the middle of it, in the apartments of the Villa Kennedy housing project.

His family was poor, with both his parents working to make ends meet. His mother worked as a manicurist, while his father was a respected studio drummer, accompanying some of the greatest salsa and bachata bands of Puerto Rico. But his father was also an alcoholic and could become violent when drunk, although Daddy Yankee doesn't give details when he talks about his childhood. To this day, Daddy Yankee does not drink, having seen the effect alcohol had on his family.

Life in the barrio was rough, but it was a life any up-and-coming rapper would envy for its richness in experience and street credibility. Despite his love of privacy, Daddy Yankee often tells about what it took to live the life he did. As he told the *New York Times*, describing the violence of the barrio:

> *"I can't tell you how many times I've woken up at three in the morning to the sound of a mother screaming and crying because she's lost her son. You learn to be a warrior here, you have no other choice."*

This was the atmosphere that shaped his childhood, for better and for worse. Daddy Yankee describes himself as "wild" in one interview, a child of the streets who, despite being smart enough to earn steady A's and B's in school, had an attitude bad enough to merit many notes home to his mother about his poor behavior. He was, in fact, such a problem to his mother that he would, years later, feel he needed to apologize for the trouble he had given her while he was growing up.

Baseball Star

Meanwhile, Ramón's first love was baseball. This was no small crush. The teenaged Ramón was convinced he was headed for the Major Leagues. His skills as a third baseman caught the attention of some scouts. Although today he is skeptical of what his chances of making it to the big time really were, young Ramón was sure it would be only a few years before he was in a ballpark somewhere in the United States, shagging flies and swinging for the bleachers. But life would take him in another direction.

Like many young boys, Ramón loved baseball—and he was good at it. He dreamed of a career in the big leagues, but fate had other plans for him.

The Turning Point

Ramón's life changed one night when he was sixteen. He was walking out of a friend's apartment when a voice shouted "Carlo!" Since his name was Ramón, after all, he ignored this. But he could not ignore what happened next. Someone raised an AK-47 and shot at Ramón. A bullet struck the would-be baseball star in the leg, shattering his *femur*.

A case of mistaken identity turned Ramón from a baseball star to a music wonder. A gunshot wound to his thigh ended any hopes that he had for a sports career.

The shooting was a case of mistaken identity, and Daddy Yankee believes the intended target was a friend of his. However, nothing could change the fact that for the next six months the once-athletic third baseman would be confined to his bed and then be unable to walk for an entire year.

Still, Daddy Yankee counts himself lucky for the experience. As he told Latina.com, "When I got shot, I was sad. But today, I thank God for that bullet. It sounds weird—nobody wants to get shot—but that was the turning point in my life."

Being shot and unable to walk for a year was a life-changing event. Ramón, unable to go out and be on the streets or play on the baseball diamond, was forced to focus on his second love: music.

A Giant Caribbean Musical Collision

Besides baseball, young Ramón loved music—a new sort of music just emerging out of the Puerto Rican barrios. This new music was called reggaeton. Although reggaeton had little resemblance to Bob Marley's distinctive reggae style, it was, as the name indicates, a relative, a grandchild, you might even say. Or you might think of reggaeton as a product of a giant Caribbean musical collision.

The oldest roots of reggaeton are in Jamaica. In the United States, reggae is one voice among many—and a small one at that—but in Jamaica it is almost everything. The reggae beat, with its bewitching bass pulse, has proved incredibly popular and has worked its way into all aspects of Jamaican music. The music is always picking up new tempos and beats but keeps the strong-yet-lazy bass line. One of these variations, most popular for late-night dancing in the clubs, is dancehall, which spread from Jamaica to Panama in the late 1970s, carried on the cassette tapes and eight tracks of Jamaican workers going to find jobs along the Panama Canal.

The seeds of reggaeton were planted in the reggae sounds born in Jamaica, another Caribbean island. Workers brought the sound to Panama, and it later made its way to Puerto Rico.

Dancehall appealed to the Panamanians, and some began to make their own Panamanian dancehall music. Some of the Jamaicans in Panama began putting out their own tracks as well, influenced by the Panamanian sound. As new dancehall tapes were made, and old ones were *recut* with Spanish lyrics, some DJs began to make a name for themselves. One DJ, El General, grew famous for taking the dancehall genre and putting a Latin spin on it, making it something definitely Panamanian.

The Birth of Reggaeton

Meanwhile, in Puerto Rico, the DJ known as Vico C had returned to his native island from New York City, bringing with him the sounds of hip-hop and rap. He began to construct what would become the first Spanish-language hip-hop, and he became famous for mixing in Latin American beats and sounds with the rest of the track, creating a new Latin American sound, just as El General had done in Panama with reggae and dancehall. These collisions of musical genre with musical genre set up another collision that would soon give birth to reggaeton.

That musical collision happened somewhere in the hot and muggy city of San Juan. When Panamanian dancehall and reggae arrived in Puerto Rico, Vico C and a few other DJs incorporated the reggae beat into their recordings and rapped their Spanish lyrics over the music. The reggae beat, however, was often too slow for proper hip-hop. The Puerto Rican DJs began to stretch, speed up, and add to the dancehall beat—all the while keeping the spirit of the steady reggae backbeat Puerto Ricans now called by a Jamaican name, Dem Bow. The music that emerged—soon to be called reggaeton—owed much to both dancehall and hip-hop.

Hip-Hop

Hip-hop is really more than merely music; it also includes art, dance, speech, and fashion. Rap—hip-hop's rhyming, rhythmic music—has its roots deep in African culture and oral tradition. The earliest African Americans kept on listening to the echo of their homeland, and whether they were worshipping or working, they would play with words, using rhyme and rhythm to express themselves. These earliest forms of rap might have been called church "testimonies," schoolyard rhymes, jailhouse rhymes, and jump-rope rhymes, but they were all black Americans getting together to rap.

Modern-day rap music came to life in the early 1970s, when a Jamaican DJ known as Kool Herc tried to use his Jamaican style of DJing—which involved reciting rhymes made up on the spot over *dubbed* versions of his reggae records—at parties in the Bronx of New York City. New Yorkers weren't into reggae back then, though, so Kool Herc adapted his style by chanting over the instrumental or percussion sections of the day's popular songs. Because these instrumental and percussion breaks were relatively short, he learned to extend them indefinitely by using an audio *mixer* and two identical records to continuously replay the desired segment. Rap took off from there.

The hip-hop culture—which also included graffiti street art and break dancing—caught on so quickly because it offered young urban New Yorkers a chance to express themselves. Rap was an art form anyone could do. You didn't need a lot of money or expensive instruments to rhyme. You didn't need to take lessons. Rapping could be practiced to perfection any time, anywhere.

Hip-hop gave kids growing up in the streets something that was in short supply: hope. At a time when prejudice, poverty, and unemployment were the realities that ruled the inner city, hip-hop offered urban young people a way to excel. If they wanted to rap, they didn't have to follow a set of rules imposed on them by white authorities; the only rules they had to follow were to be original and rhyme on time to the beat of the music. Anything was possible. You could make up a rap about your girlfriend or your own skill or the man in the moon; it didn't matter. If you were laid back, you could rap at a slow pace. If you were a fast, jumpy sort of guy, you could rap at a fast pace. No two people rapped the same, even when reciting the same rhyme. Slow or fast, the smoother you

Hip-hop was born in the South Bronx section of New York City. It was a way for poor kids to have fun—and express themselves and their opinions of the world around them.

rapped, the more praise you gathered, until you became an urban hero.

Back in the 1970s, rap was like a magnet to the kids on the streets, sucking them into its boom and its beat. Today, rap is still a form of self-expression that's within urban kids' reach—and it still gets them the attention from their peers for which all adolescents yearn. By the twenty-first century, however, hip-hop was a whole lot more than just something street

DJs were important figures in the early days of hip-hop and reggaeton. Mixing, scratching, and cutting entered the vocabulary as these new forms of music became known.

kids were doing; it had also grown into a multimillion-dollar business. At the same time, it was still doing what African American music has always done—speaking out on behalf of the black community's political, social, and economic conditions.

Street Music

Like hip-hop, reggaeton was clearly music for and by the streets. Most DJs and rappers came from the barrio, from poor families and sometimes criminal backgrounds. Their lyrics reflected their lives. They wrote about the crime, the violence, and the anger in the barrios, and they wrote about escaping the barrios. They painted a picture in words of a world of money, cars, and the good life, much like the high-rolling gangsta rap of Bentleys and bling.

Like Jamaican dancehall, reggaeton was most enjoyed late at night, in the clubs and music halls of San Juan. Like hip-hop, reggaeton was also blasted from car stereos and tape decks, on street corners and in bedrooms all throughout San Juan. But the primary purpose of reggaeton was to get bodies moving on the dance floor. Most reggaeton beats were fast and made for dancing, no matter how serious and angry the lyrics were. Reggaeton fans, whatever their situation, usually just wanted to listen to music, dance, and have fun.

A Common Background

This is not, however, to say that the lyrics about life on the street had no appeal. They certainly appealed to Ramón Ayala. Before he found reggaeton, Ramón was already listening to the American hip-hop he could hear on the radio and see on television. Although he could not understand the English lyrics, he recognized the common background he shared with the hip-hop artists.

However, Ramón still felt there was nothing similar to American hip-hop that Puerto Ricans could really call their own. For all the similarities he had with hip-hop and hip-hop artists, the music was not of the barrio, and so it could not, he felt, truly speak for him. When Ramón first heard reggaeton, he finally found a type of music he could really relate to, one that had a significant effect on him from the first time he heard it. He tells about that first time with words someone would use to describe a religious conversion: "That was it. It was real." Reggaeton—music with an irresistible beat and lyrics that spoke of life on the street and the desire to escape that life—became the second love of Ramón Ayala.

Ramón was only thirteen when he first heard reggaeton, and the music grabbed him hard. He had already been singing at parties, making up words about the people there as he went along. Soon, people started asking him to sing. Once he heard reggaeton, his singing became rapping, and he expanded beyond simply performing for friends at parties. Inspired by the American rappers he liked so much, he gave himself a nickname, a street name that implied riches and power. This is how Ramón Ayala became Daddy Yankee.

Making a Name

As Daddy Yankee began to lay down tracks and perform in clubs, his experience with *improvisation* helped him earn a name both as a talented freestyler and an overall rapper. A few of his tracks started circulating on cassette tapes sold on street corners, then booming over the sound systems of a few dance clubs in the barrio, and his popularity began to rise. Although he was nowhere near the *mainstream,* and the majority of Puerto Ricans paid no attention to reggaeton, Daddy Yankee was good enough to make a name for himself among other reggaeton artists. He was even good enough, and lucky enough, to start appearing on mix tapes by DJ Playero.

DJ Playero was a local San Juan reggaeton player, a DJ and MC who had become well known by getting barrio talent to perform, a track at a time, on mix tapes that he recorded in the living room of his apartment. Although many artists contributed to each production, it was regarded as an important and lucky event to be included on a Playero mix tape. Playero was highly regarded for his good taste and uncanny eye for talent—something that would later earn him even more fame, since many of the most famous reggaeton artists in Puerto Rico first appeared on a Playero mix tape.

It was Playero's apartment that Daddy Yankee had visited the night he had his fateful encounter with the bullet.

Once Daddy Yankee decided that music would be his career, he hit the career path running. It didn't take long before his name had become synonymous with reggaeton.

3

The Music

Not until he knew he would never play baseball again did Daddy Yankee begin to take reggaeton seriously. The doctors could not remove the bullet from his leg, and they had to replace and reinforce the remains of his femur with an awkward steel rod. Even when Daddy Yankee could finally get up and walk, it was with a limp. All that was left for him, in his mind, was the music.

Serious About the Music

Before the shooting, Daddy Yankee had laid down a track or two here, another there, spacing them out over a period of months with no great drive behind them. Now he set for himself the goal of recording an entire album, one professionally finished and polished. Once he was back on his feet, he finished it in less than a year. He released his first album, *No Mercy*, in 1995, complete with a picture of Daddy Yankee featured prominently on the cover.

On the cover, Daddy Yankee is shown standing against a clear blue sky, looking off into the distance. The cover suggests looking into the future, and Daddy Yankee was certainly doing just that. Success through reggaeton had become his only goal, and he was willing to give all he had to reach it. This meant lots of time in one makeshift studio after another, working to turn beats into bridges and finally into entire songs. But Daddy Yankee also applied his drive to succeed in other important ways.

Getting an Education

Five years went by between the release of *No Mercy* and Daddy Yankee's next album. In that time, he had been making music and performing live when he could, but most of his time had been spent at college. Daddy Yankee graduated in 1998, with a degree in finance. He chose his degree with a successful musical career in mind. If he were to navigate the world of record labels and album deals, or even reach it at all, Daddy Yankee believed he needed to speak and understand the language of money, and he did what he could to learn about it.

An Album a Year

El Cartel, Daddy Yankee's first album since *No Mercy*, was released in 2000, and others soon followed. With college out of the way now, and a firm knowledge of what the music business took, Daddy Yankee began to release an album every year, with *El Cartel II* appearing in 2001. As his rate of production rose, so did Daddy Yankee's popularity. He already had a strong reputation in San Juan, and his fame began to spread to the rest of Puerto Rico, the Puerto Rican communities in New York and other major East Coast cities in the United States, and beyond.

While he was still nowhere near mainstream in the United States, Daddy Yankee was getting noticed. His 2002 album, *El Changri*, reached #13 on the *Billboard* charts for Latin

Soon, Daddy Yankee was releasing an album a year. His name—and his talent—became known outside of his native Puerto Rico. Daddy Yankee was now an international star.

pop album. This was a victory for both Daddy Yankee and reggaeton as a whole; before his charting, most albums on the *Billboard* Latin pop charts were from more mainstream and traditional Mexican and South American musical genres.

By the early 2000s, Daddy Yankee was not only in the mainstream in Puerto Rico, he defined it. His popularity in his home country, already respectable, exploded with the release of *El Changri*. Before this album, a live show for Daddy

With his phenomenal success, Daddy Yankee was able to leave the poverty-stricken home of his youth. He moved his family to a better part of San Juan, and he's held onto his apartment there. Today, he is a frequent visitor to his hometown.

Yankee was at an upscale club or small theater. The shows would be nearly full, but the **venues** were still small. After the release of *El Changri*, Daddy Yankee played in Roberto Clemente Coliseum in San Juan for a crowd of twelve thousand enthusiastic fans. Not only did Daddy Yankee appear in the largest venue in all of Puerto Rico, but also the show more than sold out; the number of tickets sold far exceeded the official seating capacity of ten thousand. Not that anyone would be sitting. Not for reggaeton!

Some thought Daddy Yankee had nowhere left to go. He was, after all, squarely at the top of the charts in Puerto Rico. Every nightclub in San Juan, at some point during the night, shook the house with the snapping reggaeton beat that was the lifeblood of his music. All he could do now, perhaps, was continue to enjoy his success and reap in the money from record sales. But, as everyone would soon see, Daddy Yankee still had places to go.

Rising Success

The reception to Daddy Yankee's next album hinted at where he was headed. *Los Homerun-es* was a smash hit in Puerto Rico, of course, but it also sold well in the United States, well enough to reach the respectable rank of 137 on the general *Billboard* charts. And this was just the beginning.

The most important day in Daddy Yankee's career, and the most important day in the history of reggaeton, was July 13, 2004. This was the release date of *Barrio Fino*, Daddy Yankee's fifth album. As a collection of reggaeton music, *Barrio Fino* was special. For the first time, Daddy Yankee collaborated with the Dominican duo known as Luny Tunes. Together they produced an album praised by the Puerto Rican press as "original" and "progressive."

More important than the album as a whole, however, was one particular song, track five. "Gasolina" was an upbeat, traditional reggaeton tune meant to boom across a crowded

Like hip-hop, reggaeton moved out of its home base and spread around the world. Today, fans all over the world are able to download and listen to Daddy Yankee's songs on their mp3 players.

dance floor at three in the morning with its catchy refrain and irresistible beat. But this was not just another dance song.

Taking Reggaeton to the World

"Gasolina" proved a chart-shattering hit, and not only in Puerto Rico. The song began playing on radio stations throughout Latin America and the Caribbean, in places and countries where reggaeton had barely been heard before. Even in Mexico, which traditionally listened to Mexican artists only, Daddy Yankee's dance single was a hit. The popularity of the song spread from Mexico into the Mexican populations in the United States. Soon the entire Latino population of the United States was blasting "Gasolina" from car stereos and nightclub sound systems.

The real importance of "Gasolina" and *Barrio Fino*, however, was that everyone who heard it liked it. It didn't just appeal to Latinos, but to whites and blacks as well. Soon, Daddy Yankee was not only popular with the Latino population of the United States, but with much of the entire country. *Barrio Fino* easily took first place on the *Billboard* charts for Latin music, and got as a high as twenty-six on the general *Billboard* charts. To climb so high on the general charts, competing with every other artist and musical genre imaginable, Daddy Yankee needed to have a wide appeal. People who did not speak or understand a word of Spanish—beyond, maybe, the first ten numbers in Spanish that Big Bird had taught them on *Sesame Street*—bought this album.

And Americans weren't the only ones who bought the album. Daddy Yankee's popularity pushed his music across the Atlantic as well. Sales of *Barrio Fino* did far better than anyone expected in Europe. The album reached number fifty-six on the charts in France, twenty-eight in Switzerland, and fifty-one in Germany. Daddy Yankee had gone from the San Juan barrio to the world, and he had taken reggaeton with him.

Though his career started in small clubs in Puerto Rico, Daddy Yankee now draws in major crowds in venues all over the world.

4

The Man

International popularity has certainly changed Ramón Ayala's life. He doesn't live in Las Lomas anymore, for one thing. Daddy Yankee still lives in San Juan, but now he has his own house in the wealthy neighborhood of Isla Verde. When he travels, it's to give a concert in Madison Square Garden, or to do a photo shoot for his music label or his clothing line in Los Angeles, or to work with another artist on putting together a track for a new album. He flies first class, stays in five-star hotels, and is always surrounded by the beat of his music coming from radio and car stereos.

Then there are the fans. Even at home in San Juan, he has to sign autographs and pose for pictures wherever he goes. Daddy Yankee only has to walk down the street in San Juan, New York,

Mexico City, Bogotá, or any number of places, and he hears his name screamed out by passersby, sounding like it does on "Gasolina."

"DAH! DI! YAN! KEE!"

The Price of Fame

Fame isn't always a good thing, though. It nearly cost him an ear once.

On his first trip to Colombia, Daddy Yankee spent some time out on the streets of Bogotá, signing autographs. The screams and excitement were normal, until one particular Colombian fan got a little too excited. Shrieking and squealing, she apparently decided she just had to touch the reggaeton star she loved so much. For some reason, she decided the best place to touch him would be his ear. Daddy Yankee remembers her as being hysterical, crazy with excitement, holding tighter and tighter to his ear.

At this point, the people with Daddy Yankee—there to keep him safe and hold his cell phone—started to get a little worried. The fan would not let go, not once she had finally gotten a grip on her idol. Instead, the weakest link in the tug of war turned out to be Daddy Yankee's ear. Who knows what the screaming fan thought as her hand tore Daddy Yankee's ear from his head, but she apparently realized what she had done. Daddy Yankee was able to get the ear back in time to have it reattached during emergency surgery.

Daddy Yankee isn't angry at the fan for what she did. He says he understands the situation she was in. He understands that he is incredibly famous, especially in the Latino world, and the power fame has over people. But how does he react to this? What does Ramón Ayala, born and raised in one of the poorest, roughest sections of San Juan, think of it all, and how does he think he should deal with it?

Life is good for Daddy Yankee. He travels, playing concerts in such famous venues as Madison Square Garden. Plus, he's got his own clothing line—DY. He's worked hard to achieve all that he has.

Keeping in Touch with the Barrio

To Daddy Yankee, it's important to "keep it real." This phrase is often used by hip-hop artists, movie stars, athletes, and anyone else who has used some special talent to rise from poverty to riches. Hip-hop artists, especially, are afraid that if they don't keep in touch with their upbringing, their life before they became rich and moved out of the projects, they'll lose

When Daddy Yankee flies, it's first class all the way. But that doesn't mean he stays in the first-class section of the airplane. When he runs out of people to talk to there, he wanders around the plane to find other eager listeners. His flights are never boring!

their credibility, their ability to rap about life on the streets and be taken seriously. Daddy Yankee shares this concern and does what he can to keep hold of his background. As he put it in an interview with the *New York Times*, "The street is my inspiration. If I lose it, I lose my music."

So Daddy Yankee is careful to make sure he does not lose Ramón Ayala in the rush of wealth and fame that comes with being a reggaeton star. He keeps his connection to the barrio as much as he can, rooting himself like a tree in the life he lived growing up.

One of Daddy Yankee's two main managers is his brother Nomar, who goes with him everywhere, keeping him in touch with both the record companies and his family back home. His other manager is his wife, Mirredys. They got married when they were only seventeen and lived together in a three-room apartment in Villa Kennedy. Now they divide their time between San Juan, their three children, and wherever Daddy Yankee's career takes them. When Daddy Yankee mentions Mirredys in interviews, he describes her as his touchstone, who laughs when his lady fans go crazy over him and reminds him constantly of the times they had together in their small apartment.

Daddy Yankee still owns that three-room apartment. "The first thing that I do when I get back from traveling," he says, "is go home, take a shower, and drive over to my neighborhood." He goes back to Villa Kennedy regularly, just to relax and be in a place where people still remember Ramón Ayala. He goes there to maintain his connection with his past and his people, and while Villa Kennedy is not his first home anymore, it is at least his second. It's where he goes to be Ramón again, where people chide him to spend his money well and not allow himself to get too comfortable with fame and fortune, reminding him instead that they remember him as he was before the fame or even the gunshot: a little poor boy with a big mouth.

Using Fame to Help

Daddy Yankee's connection to Puerto Rico is deeper than the occasional visit to Villa Kennedy. His actions as a reggaeton star make it clear that he still has ties to those in the barrio, especially to the children. Not only does he use the barrio to escape his fame, he also uses his fame to help the barrio. Of all the reggaeton stars to come out of San Juan, or Puerto Rico as a whole, Daddy Yankee was the first to offer free concerts to barrio children. He started the free concerts before *Barrio Fino* was ever published and continues them to this day, filling entire stadiums with kids from the projects.

Beyond the free concerts, Daddy Yankee is also very active in San Juan's charities. He uses his fame to give joy to his less fortunate fans and his money to help with needed food and supplies. For example, Daddy Yankee visited a barrio school for children with special needs to talk to the kids, sign autographs, shake hands, and let the students experience the awe that comes from meeting someone as famous as Daddy Yankee. He also brought gifts with him, things the school needed very much. These included things like computers, books, paper, and pencils, but also things only someone who had grown up in San Juan would know to get for a school—such as fans and watercoolers to help deal with the heavy Caribbean heat.

Breaking the Cycle

Daddy Yankee has even established his own foundation to help people in the barrio. The foundation, which he has named Fundación Corazón Guerrero, or Warrior Heart Foundation, is aimed at kids, particularly teenagers, who are returning to the barrio from jail. Before these kids leave prison, Daddy Yankee hopes, the foundation will give them an education they can use once they're out. When they are released, the foundation will give them a place to stay if they need it, as well as provide counseling and help finding a job. Daddy Yankee's intention is to break the cycle of violence he feels consumes the streets of San Juan: young people who commit crimes go to jail where they are exposed to an intense criminal **culture** and are then released feeling they have no option but to continue a life of crime.

The foundation shares its name with the song "Corazónes" that appeared on *Barrio Fino*. This song differs sharply from the other songs on the album; its beat is far calmer and its intent far more serious. The music videos made for the other

Despite the trappings that come with success, Daddy Yankee hasn't forgotten his roots. He often visits schools in the poverty-stricken barrio. His foundation also provides help for young people living there.

To most in the music industry, piracy is an evil. That's not necessarily true for Daddy Yankee. He'd rather his fans who couldn't afford to buy a commercial CD have a cheaper version of his music than none at all. But that's as far as his support of piracy goes.

songs on the album are bright, colorful, and full of dancers, while the video for "Corazónes" is very dark, focusing only on Daddy Yankee, who stands behind a podium, singing like he's giving a speech to the audience. Daddy Yankee sings about his fears that the culture of the Puerto Rico barrio has become one of violence and death. He ends the song with a call for peace between gangs, and for the people of the barrio to try to make their lives better.

Is Music Piracy Ever OK?

Daddy Yankee's desire to help the barrio poor goes beyond his own charities. In one controversial example, Daddy Yankee said he actually supported, in a few cases, music *piracy*, even of his own songs and CDs. The price of CDs was high enough, he said, that truly poor people could not spare the money to buy them. He was bothered that some of his fans could not afford to enjoy his music the way he would like them to be able to. In that situation, Daddy Yankee said, he would prefer that fans purchase a much cheaper pirated version of his music than simply go without. He was quick to make it clear that he only supported music piracy in situations where those buying the pirated music could not otherwise afford it. If you had the spare money for a CD, then, "Why don't you just, you know, buy the CD?"

People Person

While Daddy Yankee's first interest is the people of the barrios, he is open to all his fans. Unlike some artists who sometimes travel with an *entourage* that looks like a small army—including everyone from swanky publicists to giant security guards—Daddy Yankee only brings along a group of five or fewer, a group that never includes any security at all. There is nothing and no one to separate Daddy Yankee from his fans, and that's how he likes it. If he has the time, he will get his picture taken, give an autograph, or just say hello to any fan

Daddy Yankee sees himself as more than a musician. He considers himself the voice and face of Latinos all over the world, an ambassador for his people.

who comes up to him. Even when he does not exactly want to deal with fans, Daddy Yankee makes barely any effort to hide from them. At a baseball game, for example, he might try to disguise himself by wearing a hat and sunglasses, and maybe by sitting near the top of the stands so fewer people can see him. Nothing more.

The truth is, Daddy Yankee loves to meet new people, and just be around other people in general. He told Reuters in an interview that on airplanes, he'll fly first class, but often ends up in coach when he runs out of people to talk to in the front. He explains this personality quirk as something left over from life in the barrio, where you needed to have as many friends and people to help you as you could. Wherever he goes now, Daddy Yankee still loves being friendly and in touch with his fans.

Daddy Yankee is more than just a *philanthropist* or a good example of a humble, friendly star. He has taken on another role as well, one that springs from his position as one of the pioneers of international reggaeton. His mission is to be a voice and a face for Latinos the world over, from Mexico to New York to Puerto Rico to Argentina.

Latino culture is spreading around the world. Music—and musicians such as Daddy Yankee—truly speak an international language.

The Mission

5

Daddy Yankee seeks to create proper respect for Latino culture and spread parts of that culture—in particular the music—to the rest of the world. He welcomes his role as a cultural *icon* for Latinos, particularly for those living in the United States. For him, reggaeton is more than just a musical fad, a craze that will soon fade into the bargain bin and die there, as some music critics and newspapers have been whispering. Rather, Daddy Yankee sees reggaeton as only the tip of the iceberg that is the rising Latino culture.

When he made his grand entrance into Madison Square Garden on the first night of a nationwide arena tour—playing to crowds numbering tens of thousands in the largest and most important venues in the country—Daddy Yankee shouted to the crowd over and over, with his fist in the air, "We're ready! We're ready!" With that rallying cry, Daddy Yankee spoke for the Latino community, stating that it was time for the Latino culture to stop being influenced by others and to take its place in the world. As the biggest name in reggaeton, the most influential trend to come out of Latin America in living memory, Daddy Yankee is in the perfect position to lead Latino culture forward.

Ever since the release of *Barrio Fino*, leading Latino culture forward is exactly what Daddy Yankee has been doing. As the

Though he's not as well known outside of Puerto Rico as Daddy Yankee, Don Omar is gaining popularity in the United States. In this photo, he is shown at the 2006 Annual Puerto Rican Day Parade in New York City.

creator of the hit song "Gasolina," which introduced reggaeton to an unsuspecting world, Daddy Yankee broke the market open for the other reggaeton artists of Puerto Rico and elsewhere. While Daddy Yankee was the first success, moving from a Puerto Rican star to global superstar status, others are right behind him. Though no one is as popular outside the Spanish-speaking world as Daddy Yankee, artists like Don Omar, Ivy Queen, Calle 13, and Luny Tunes are all following the path to global popularity and success that Daddy Yankee has blazed.

Reggaeton in the Mainstream

Reggaeton itself, meanwhile, is perhaps doing even better than Daddy Yankee himself. In areas of the United States with large Latino populations, entire radio stations that before played jazz, rock, or even hip-hop, now play reggaeton. Radio corporations like Clear Channel call the format "Hurban," a word that is a combination of "Hispanic" and "Urban." Daddy Yankee even has his own radio show, distributed to radio stations all over the United States by ABC. Naturally, it is devoted to reggaeton, with Daddy Yankee presenting a selection of new and upcoming reggaeton artists and their music.

Reggaeton is not played only by Puerto Rican, or even Latin American, artists anymore, either. Other artists have seen the success of Daddy Yankee and reggaeton as a whole and are now trying their hand at the Dem Bow beat. Many of these artists are Latinos themselves and are for the first time rapping in the language their parents speak. Some though, like Lil Jon or Mary J. Blige, do not come from a Latino heritage at all but have still experimented with Spanish lyrics. Mary J. Blige liked the response to the few Spanish songs she included on an album so much that she plans to do an entirely Spanish version of her next album.

The Future of Reggaeton

Despite this ongoing victory for reggaeton, Daddy Yankee is still not satisfied. Not only does he want to see reggaeton succeed and expand, he also wants to see it evolve, to grow into something better and hopefully even longer lasting. He has said, in fact, that after reaching the mainstream, reggaeton **stagnated**, with artists producing songs with beats and themes too much like other songs; no one was really trying to reach for a new sound. Daddy Yankee aims to change that, something that he says his 2007 album, *El Cartel: The Big Boss*, will do.

For Daddy Yankee, this means in part a move deeper into the mainstream. *El Cartel*, Daddy Yankee has said, will have some songs done less with the style and beat of traditional reggaeton and rather with a beat more similar to hip-hop or **R&B**. Other songs will feature or be produced by major hip-hop artists, including Snoop Dogg, Fergie and Will.i.am of the Black Eyed Peas, and Nicole Scherzinger of the Pussycat Dolls.

At the same time, Daddy Yankee is also committed to keeping the album true to his roots and the roots of reggaeton. Although parts of the album will be in English, Spanish will still be the main language of Daddy Yankee's music. Also, while plenty of songs will be fit for shaking up the club at two in the morning, *El Cartel* will also feature some of what Daddy Yankee calls "Protest Rap"—songs in the style of "Corazónes," sung with strength and anger about problems facing those still trapped by poverty.

Even a Clothing Line

As for the rest of Latino culture, the underwater iceberg that is ready to rise, Daddy Yankee is right there rising with it. Not only does he have his own radio show, but he also has his own Reebok shoe and a clothing line called DY. The logo is simply

Some people, including Daddy Yankee, think that reggaeton hit a standstill after it reached the music mainstream. But Daddy Yankee isn't going to let it stay there. He's working hard to create music that will help the genre grow.

the letters DY in uppercase, looking similar to the famous N and Y of the New York Yankees. Although a clothing line may seem to have little to do with the rise of Latino culture, and more to do with the ego of a music star and a clothing company cashing in on his fame, Daddy Yankee makes even the clothes he helps sell connect to the barrio and his upbringing.

In keeping with his dedication to Latinos as a group, the slogan of Daddy Yankee's clothing line is "For the People"—a

Reggaeton, like hip-hop, is music for the people. It tells their stories in ways everyone can relate. That's what Daddy Yankee has done in the past, and it's what he vows to keep doing.

kind of mission statement for the product. Daddy Yankee does not just want to create clothing, he wants to give Latinos a line of street clothing to call their own, much like Fubu or Nike is the clothing of choice for urban America.

The shoe that forms the cornerstone of the Daddy Yankee clothing empire reflects this goal. At first glance, the shoe looks much like any other urban shoe, but it is undoubtedly Latino. The inside of the shoe even bears a map of Latin America, stretching from Mexico and the Caribbean in the heel all the way down to Chile and Argentina by the toe. Daddy Yankee does not try to hide that he is a businessman in the tradition of other hip-hop starts like Sean Combs or Jay Z, but he still remains dedicated to the idea of creating a stronger, more unique identity for Latinos.

Daddy Yankee's mission of spreading and strengthening Latino culture has not gone unnoticed. Of all the awards that Daddy Yankee has received, none are more complementary, or more important, than the one he received on May 8, 2006. In recognition of his fame, his trailblazing for reggaeton, and his help for Latino culture in general, *Time* magazine included Daddy Yankee in its 2006 "Time 100" list of "The People Who Shape Our World." The list also included people like Bill Clinton, George H. W. Bush, George W. Bush, and John McCain.

From the barrio, Ramón Ayala has brought himself to the highest ranks of our culture. What's more, he shows no sign of stopping!

**Late
1970s**   Ramón Ayala, the future Daddy Yankee, is born in Puerto Rico.

Reggae spreads from Jamaica to Panama.

1995   *No Mercy*, Daddy Yankee's first album, is released.

1998   Daddy Yankee graduates from college with a degree in finance.

2000   *El Cartel* is released.

2001   *El Cartel II* is released.

2002   *El Changri* hits the *Billboard* Latin charts.

2003   *Los Homerun-es* ranks on the *Billboard* general charts.

2004   *Barrio Fino* is released.

Appears in the film *Vampiros*.

2005   *Barrio Fino* is nominated for multiple *Billboard* awards, winning Best Latin Music Album of the Year.

Barrio Fino wins the Latin Grammy for Best Urban Music Album.

2006   Daddy Yankee wins another *Billboard* Music Award.

Daddy Yankee is named by *Time* magazine one of the People Who Shape Our World.

Forms his own clothing company, DY.

His first shoe is released by Reebok.

2007 *El Cartel: The Big Boss* is released.

Appears in the film *Talento de Barrio*.

Albums

1995   *No Mercy*

1996   *El Yankee 2*

2000   *El Cartel*

2001   *El Cartel II*

2002   *El Cangri.com*

Awards

2004   *New York Times*: Names *Barrio Fino* one of the best hip-hop albums of the year.

2005   *Billboard* Latin Music Award: Reggaeton Album of the Year.

2006   Latin Grammy Awards: Best Urban Music Album (*Barrio Fino*); *Billboard* Latin Music Awards: Reggaeton Album of the Year (*Barrio Fino*), Latin Album Artist of the Year, Reggaeton Song of the Year ("Mayor Que Yo"); MTV Music Awards Latin America: Artist of the Year.

Books and Articles

Castillo-Garstow, Melissa. "Latinos in Hip Hop to Reggaeton." *Latin Beat*, 2005.

du Lac, J. Freedom. "Daddy and His Brand New Bag." *Washington Post*, August 14, 2005.

Emerick, Laura. "Reggaeton Comes Up from the Underground: Daddy Yankee Leads the Way." *Chicago-Sun Times*, March 13, 2005.

Kallen, Stuart A. *The History of Latin Music*. Farmington Hills, Mich.: Thomson Gale, 2006.

Levin, Jordan. "Reggaeton Gets Rich—and Rapper Daddy Yankee Leads the Way." *Miami Herald*, March 11, 2005.

Myrie, Russell. "He's the Daddy! Meet the RUN DMC of Reggaeton, Daddy Yankee." *Voice*, August 7, 2005.

"The Time 100: The People Who Shape Our World." *Time*, 2006 (http://www.time.com/time/magazine/article/0,9171,1187400,00.html).

Waters, Rosa. *Hip-Hop: A Short History*. Broomall, Pa.: Mason Crest, 2007.

Daddy Yankee
www.mtv.com/music/artist/yankee_daddy/artist.jhtml

Daddy Yankee/El Cartel/The Big Boss
www.daddyyankee.com

Daddy Yankee on MySpace
www.myspace.com/daddyyankee

Music of Puerto Rico
www.musicofpuertorico.com/index.php/artists/
daddy_yankee

Reggaeton History
www.tqnyc.org/NYC063107/reggaeton_history.htm

Reggaeton Online
www.reggaetonline.net

Glossary

anthems—Songs that serve as themes for a nation or social movement.

barrio—A Spanish-speaking neighborhood in a city or town.

bling—Jewelry that is big and shiny.

culture—The shared beliefs, customs, practices, and social behavior of a particular nation or people.

dubbed—Remixed records to bring some instruments into the foreground and causing others to echo.

entourage—A group of special employees who go with high-profile people on visits and engagements.

femur—The main bone in the human thigh.

gangsta rapper—A performer who raps songs in which the lyrics tend to deal with gangs and killings.

genre—One of the categories into which artistic works can be divided into on the basis of form, style, or subject matter.

icon—Someone widely and uncritically admired, especially someone symbolizing a movement or field of activity.

improvisation—Something performed without preparation.

mainstream—The ideas, actions, and values that are most widely accepted by a group or society.

mixer—A machine that adjusts and combines various inputs to create a single output.

philanthropist—Someone who desires to improve the material, social, and spiritual welfare of humanity, especially through charitable activities.

piracy—The taking and using of copyrighted or patented material without authorization or without the legal right to do so.

R&B—Rhythm and blues, a genre of music that typically includes elements of blues and African-American folk music, marked by a strong beat and simple chord structure.

recut—To re-record a song.

salsa—A type of Latin American dance music that combines elements of jazz and rock with African-Cuban melodies.

stagnated—Failed to develop past a particular point.

venues—Locations of events.

Index

About the Author

Nat Cotts first encountered reggaeton booming from car stereos on the streets of Cuautla, Mexico, and he has been keeping an ear to the music of that movement ever since. He has enjoyed writing about the phenomenon, and he can't wait to see where it goes next.

Picture Credits

Harris, Glenn / PR Photos: p. 47
iStockphoto:
    Besser, Michal: p. 23
    Ergan, Hasan Kursad: p. 18
    Feurich, Andree: p. 40
    Gonzalez, Guillermo Perales: p. 48
    Govorushchenko, Kateryna: p. 34
    Grove, Bill: p. 36
    Gumerov, Alex: p. 24
    Hamda, Wael: p. 44
    Jacob, Bonnie: p. 54
    Laufenberg, Brandon: p. 43
    Marlow, Bradley L.: p. 16
    McCaig, Tim: p. 20
    Podgorsek, Simon: p. 11
    Sawyer, Lawrence: pp. 14, 32
    Zivana, Ufuk: p. 12
Mayer, Janet/PR Photos: front cover, pp. 2, 8, 28, 31, 39, 50, 53

To the best knowledge of the publisher, all other images are in the public domain. If any image has been inadvertently uncredited, please notify Harding House Publishing Service, Vestal, New York 13850, so that rectification can be made for future printings.